ALMOST CHRISTMAS
A Wesleyan Advent Experience
Leader Guide

ALMOST CHRISTMAS

A Wesleyan Advent Experience

ALMOST CHRISTMAS
978-1-5018-9057-4

ALMOST CHRISTMAS: DVD
978-1-5018-9062-8

ALMOST CHRISTMAS: LEADER GUIDE
978-1-5018-9060-4

ALMOST CHRISTMAS: YOUTH STUDY BOOK
978-1-5018-9067-3

ALMOST CHRISTMAS: DEVOTIONS
978-1-5018-9069-7

ALSO FROM MAGREY R. DEVEGA
Awaiting the Already
Embracing the Uncertain

ALSO FROM MATT RAWLE
The Redemption of Scrooge
The Gift of the Nutcracker
What Makes a Hero?
The Grace of Les Misérables

ALMOST CHRISTMAS

A WESLEYAN ADVENT EXPERIENCE

MAGREY R. DEVEGA · INGRID MCINTYRE
APRIL CASPERSON · MATT RAWLE

LEADER GUIDE

Abingdon Press
Nashville

Almost Christmas
A Wesleyan Advent Experience
Leader Guide

Copyright © 2019 by Abingdon Press
All rights reserved.

ISBN-13: 978-1-5018-9060-4

19 20 21 22 23 24 25 26 27 28—10 9 8 7 6 5 4 3 2 1
MANUFACTURED IN THE UNITED STATES OF AMERICA

CONTENTS

*Special thanks to The New Room in Bristol, UK,
and to David Worthington, Director of the
New Room, for providing four bonus videos for
the Almost Christmas DVD, exploring the lives of
John and Charles Wesley in the context of Advent.*

*The New Room is the oldest Methodist building
in the world. Visit them online at:*
www.newroombristol.org.uk

Additional resources, including Advent and Nativity hymn suggestions, litanies for lighting the Advent wreath, and prayers that can be used in worship and small group settings are available at **https://www.abingdonpress.com /Almost-Christmas-Downloads**.

TO THE LEADER

Welcome! Thank you for accepting the invitation to serve as the facilitator for this study of *Almost Christmas: A Wesleyan Advent Experience*. During this study you and your group of learners will come to an understanding of what it means to move from having an "Almost Christmas" to having an "Altogether Christmas."

This leader guide contains four session plans based on the four chapters in *Almost Christmas*:

- "An Altogether Peace" by Magrey R. deVega,
- "An Altogether Hope" by Ingrid McIntyre,
- "An Altogether Love" by April Casperson, and
- "An Altogether Joy" by Matt Rawle.

These four authors draw on Scripture and the writings of John and Charles Wesley as they consider God's gifts of peace, hope, love, and joy.

This Leader Guide also contains plans for an optional fifth session with the liturgy and instructions for celebrating "A Service of Covenant Renewal" together. You may want to schedule this fifth session for after Christmas as a way to observe the beginning of a new calendar year.

This study makes use of the following components:

- the book *Almost Christmas: A Wesleyan Advent Experience*,
- this Leader Guide, and
- a DVD with video segments for each of the four chapters in the book.

It will be helpful if participants obtain a copy of *Almost Christmas* in advance and read the introduction and first chapter before the first session. Each participant will also need a Bible. It is recommended that participants have a notebook or journal for taking notes, recording insights, and noting questions during the study.

Session Format

Every group is different. These session plans have been designed to give you flexibility and choices. A variety of activities and discussion questions is included. As you plan each session, keep the session goals in mind and select the activities and discussion questions that will be most meaningful for your group.

You will want to read the section titled "Before the Session" several days in advance of your meeting time. A few activities suggest making some preparations in advance.

The activities in "Getting Started" are designed to help participants begin to focus on the main topics for the session. They also serve as group building exercises. Watch your time here so you will have time for the in-depth study later in the session.

In many cases, your session time will be too short to do everything that is suggested here. Keeping the personality of your group in mind and the specific aspects of each chapter you want to focus on, decide ahead of time which activities and discussion questions you want to include in the session and how much time you want to allow for each. The "Optional Activities" give you the opportunity to do more in-depth study of a particular topic.

The activities in "Wrapping Up" are designed to give participants the opportunity to reflect on and process the various themes and topics covered in the session, as these relate to their own growing relationship with Jesus Christ. A "Closing Prayer" is provided. Feel free to offer your own prayer instead.

Each session plan follows this outline:

Planning the Session
- Session Goals
- Biblical Foundation
- Before the Session

Getting Started
- Opening Activities
- Opening Prayer

Learning Together
- Video Study and Discussion
- Bible Study and Discussion
  (In Session 1, the Bible Study follows the Book Study.)
- Book Study and Discussion
- Optional Activity or Activities

Wrapping Up
- Closing Activity
- Closing Prayer

Preparing for the Session

Here are some helpful guidelines and suggestions for helping you prepare to lead this study and each session.

- Pray for the Holy Spirit to lead you as you prepare for the study. Pray for discernment for yourself and for each member of the study group.
- Before each session, familiarize yourself with the content. Read the book chapter again and watch the video segment for that session.
- Choose the session elements you will use during the group session, including the specific discussion questions you plan to cover. Be prepared, however, to adjust the session as group members interact and as questions arise. Prepare carefully, but allow space for the Holy Spirit to move in and through the material, the group members, and you as facilitator.

- Secure in advance a TV and DVD player or a computer with projection capabilities so that you can play the video session for your group.
- Prepare the space so that it will enhance the learning process. Ideally, group members should be seated around a table or in a circle so that all can see one another. Movable chairs are best, because the group will often be forming pairs or small groups for discussion.
- Bring a supply of Bibles for those who forget to bring their own. It is helpful to have several different translations.
- For each session you will also need a markerboard and markers, a chalkboard and chalk, or an easel with paper and markers.

Shaping the Learning Environment

The following are a few tips for guiding your group to allow for the best possible discussion and engagement in the session each week.

- Begin and end on time.
- Create a climate of openness, encouraging group members to participate as they feel comfortable. Remember that some people will jump right in with answers and comments, while others will need time to process what is being discussed.
- If you notice that some group members don't enter the conversation, ask them if they have thoughts to share. Give everyone a chance to talk, but keep the conversation moving. Try to prevent a few individuals from doing all the talking.
- Communicate the importance of group discussions and group exercises.
- If no one answers at first during discussions, don't be afraid of pauses. Count silently to ten; then say something such as "Would anyone like to go first?" If no one responds, venture an answer yourself and ask for comments.

- Model openness as you share with the group. Group members will follow your example. If you limit your sharing to a surface level, others will follow suit.
- Encourage multiple answers or responses before moving on.
- Ask, "Why?" or "Why do you believe that?" or "Can you say more about that?" to help continue a discussion and give it greater depth.
- Affirm others' responses with comments such as "Great" or "Thanks" or "Good insight"—especially if this is the first time someone has spoken during the group session.
- Monitor your own contributions. If you find yourself doing most of the talking, back off so that you don't train the group to listen rather than speak up.
- Remember that you don't have all the answers. Your job is to keep the discussion going and encourage participation.

Managing the Session

- Honor the time schedule. If a session is running longer than expected, get consensus from the group before continuing beyond the agreed-upon ending time.
- Involve group members in various aspects of the group session, such as playing the DVD, saying prayers, or reading the Scripture.
- Note that the session plans sometimes call for breaking into smaller groups. This gives everyone a chance to speak and participate fully. Mix up the teams; don't let the same people pair up on every activity.
- **CONFIDENTIALITY: Because many activities call for personal sharing, confidentiality is essential. Group members should never pass along stories that have been shared in the group. Remind the group members at each session: confidentiality is crucial to the success of this study.**

SESSION 1
AN ALTOGETHER *PEACE*

By MAGREY R. DEVEGA

Planning the Session

Session Goals

Through conversation, activities, and reflection, participants will

- understand what the authors mean by "Almost Christmas,"
- explore John Wesley's understanding of what it means to be a peacemaker,
- affirm the fullness of Jesus' gift of peace, and
- open hearts to receive Jesus' gift of peace.

Biblical Foundation

- John 14:27; 16:33; 20:19-23
- Ephesians 4:3-6, 25-32

Before the Session

- Set up a table in the room with nametags, markers, Bibles, extra copies of *Almost Christmas*, in case anyone does not have his or her copy, and paper and pencils.
- Prepare a sign-in sheet with space for each participant's name and contact information.
- Have a markerboard or easel with paper and markers or a chalkboard and chalk available for use during the session.

13

- You may want to make four "distance and destination" signs that read Almost Peace, Almost Hope, Almost Love, and Almost Joy. Display these four signs in your meeting space throughout the study.
- Write the heading "Getting Ready for Christmas" on a board or large sheet of paper for use in "Leading into the Study."
- Write the three questions for the small group discussion described in this session plan under "Bible Study and Discussion: John and Ephesians" on a board or large sheet of paper, or make copies of the questions to distribute to each small group.
- If you want to do the Optional Activity "Silent Night," make preparations to play a recording of this hymn or secure hymnals and an accompanist so the group may sing the hymn together.

Getting Started

Greet participants as they arrive. Invite each person to make a nametag and pick up either a Bible or copy of *Almost Christmas*, or both, if necessary.

Introductions

Introduce yourself and share your hopes for the group as you study the book *Almost Christmas* together.

If the participants in your group do not know one another well, allow time for them to introduce themselves and share something about their relationship with the church—for example, the name of a Sunday school class or small group to which they belong, a mission project they support, which worship service they attend, or if they are a visitor. Extend a special welcome to anyone who does not regularly attend your church and invite them to worship if they do not have a church home.

Housekeeping

- Share any necessary information about your meeting space, parking, and the class schedule.

- Collect contact information from each participant in case you need to share information during the course, and also share your contact information with participants.
- Let the group know you will be faithful to the time and encourage everyone to arrive on time.
- Encourage everyone to read the upcoming chapter before the next session.
- You may want to invite participants to have a notebook, journal, or electronic tablet for use during this study. Explain that these can be used to record questions and insights they have as they read each chapter and to take notes during each session.
- Explain the importance of confidentiality and ask participants to covenant together to respect a policy of confidentiality within the group.
- If you plan to conclude the study with "A Service of Covenant Renewal," share information about this service including the date, time, and place. If you would like participants to assist you in leading this service (reading Scripture, leading music, serving Holy Communion), have a sign-up sheet available for volunteers. For more information about leading this service, see the instructions in the optional Session 5.

Leading into the Study

Invite participants to call out responses to the following question. Record answers on the board or large sheet of paper with the heading "Getting Ready for Christmas." Recruit a timekeeper and limit this activity to two minutes. Ask:

- What do you do to get ready for Christmas?

After the two minutes are up, briefly review the responses that you have recorded. Call attention to the opening illustration in the introduction to *Almost Christmas* and ask:

- When have you asked the question Dennis the Menace asked about Christmas, "Is that all?"

- Do you open all of your gifts under the Christmas tree and then feel that a gift is missing? If yes, what do you feel is missing? (The author makes the point that the gift that is missing is the gift of ourselves to God.)

Share key points from the introduction about (1) what it means to give ourselves to God, and (2) Wesley's sermon "The Almost Christian."

(If you would like to follow Magrey R. deVega's suggestion to pray through Wesley's twenty-five questions during this Advent season, include the Optional Activity "An Advent Prayer Calendar" in your session plan.)

Call attention to the four chapter titles in *Almost Christmas* and note that each chapter is written by a different author. The subject for this session is "Altogether Peace."

Opening Prayer

Holy God of Peace, thank you for this season of Advent, this special time of year set aside for us to prepare ourselves for the celebration of the birth of Jesus. Thank you for each person in this group. Guide our time together and help us come to a greater understanding of your gifts of peace, hope, love, and joy. Open our hearts that we may receive these gifts and experience an altogether Christmas this year; in the name of your Son Jesus we pray. Amen.

Learning Together

Video Study and Discussion

Play the video for Session 1 and invite the group to consider these questions as they view the video:

- What story or perspective in the video resonated with you the most? What challenged you? Why?
- Based on the conversation in the video, what do you see as the difference between the "almost" and the "altogether" in the Christian life?

- How can the knowledge that God is with us at all times form the basis for an altogether peace?
- The speakers in the video described the importance of community for true peace. Where do you see your community helping bring about a sense of peace for its members?
- What would help you and your community move closer to an altogether peace?

Following the video, invite volunteers to share their responses to the questions above.

Book Study and Discussion

(In this session the Bible Study and Discussion follows the Book Study and Discussion.)

Call attention to deVega's opening illustration in chapter 1 about being on a car trip. Ask:

- What two things does a roadside "distance and destination" sign tell us?
  - » We are closer to our destination than when we started.
  - » We still have a distance to travel.
- What are our four destinations as we journey to the manger during the season of Advent? *(Peace, Hope, Love, Joy)*

If you made the four "distance and destination" signs (see "Before the Session"), call attention to them now.

Note deVega's observation that we experience a "tension" during the season of Advent in that we look forward to Jesus coming again and yet we know that Jesus is already here.

We also experience a "tension" with respect to the four "destinations" of Advent. We do experience Peace, Hope, Love, and Joy; yet we know that we do not experience these to the fullest. Invite participants to consult the opening paragraphs of chapter 1 in the book and also to share personal experience as they respond to these questions. Ask:

- During the seasons of Advent and Christmas, how do you experience

  » "almost peace,"
  » "almost hope,"
  » "almost love," and
  » "almost joy"?

Share this quotation from *Almost Christmas*: "The chapters ahead will take us to some pretty deep places showing us how to claim the arrival of a God-with-us, who sees us through to the destination regardless of how long we have traveled, or how long it feels before we get there. It will help us cover the distance between *almost* and *altogether*."

Call attention to Wesley's use of the words *almost* and *altogether*. The author notes that "Wesley used that term 'almost' to describe the Christian who had the outward 'form of godliness,' but still fell short of 'altogether' godliness on the inside."

UNDERSTANDING THE CONCEPTS: It is important that participants understand the concepts of "almost" and "altogether" as these relate to Advent and God's gifts of Peace, Hope, Love, and Joy. If you feel there are still questions within your group about these concepts, pause here for further explanation and discussion before proceeding with the session plan.

Remind the group that the title for this session is "Altogether Peace." Invite participants to share examples of places where we experience a *lack* of peace or an almost peace today:

- in our world;
- in our country;
- in relationships with family, friends, coworkers;
- in our congregation;
- within ourselves.

Note the repetition of the angels' message in the Christmas stories in the Gospels of Matthew and Luke: "Do not be afraid." Invite participants to refer to Matthew 1 and 2 and Luke 1–2:20 along with the first section of chapter 1 as they respond to this question. Ask:

- Where are there examples of a lack of peace in the Christmas story as told in the Gospels of Matthew and Luke?

In the section of chapter 1 titled "Peace: Anger's Antidote," the author makes the point that fear, tension, and the chaos of the Advent/Christmas seasons may cause us to feel anger. He writes, "It's helpful to note that anger is not, in and of itself, sinful. Frustration is a natural part of life. If you've been hurt, it's natural to be angry. If you see injustice, anger is appropriate. If you are frustrated with yourself, anger happens."

Invite volunteers to share information from *Almost Christmas* about three steps for responding to anger in healthy, productive, and peaceful ways: awareness, acceptance, and action.

Ask participants to turn to the section of chapter 1 titled "Wesley: Do Good." Recruit two volunteers to read aloud the two excerpts from Wesley's sermon provided in this section. Ask:

- What is the connection between doing good and being a peacemaker?
- What challenges do you face when you seek to do good?
- Where can you be a peacemaker and make a difference?
- In what ways does John Wesley inspire you to do good and be a peacemaker?

Bible Study and Discussion: John and Ephesians

Summarize the information in the section of chapter 1 titled "John 14: Peace, Not as the World Gives" about the Roman understanding of peace prevalent in Jesus' day.

Read or recruit volunteers to read John 14:27 and John 16:33. These verses are provided below.

"Peace I leave with you. My peace I give you. I give to you not as the world gives. Don't be troubled or afraid."

(John 14:27)

*"I've said these things to you so that you will have peace in me. In
the world you have distress. But be encouraged! I have conquered
the world."*

(John 16:33)

Ask participants to refer to the section of chapter 1 titled "Shalom"
as they respond to the following questions. You may want to record
responses on a board or large sheet of paper. Ask:

- What was Jesus' understanding of peace? (Shalom)
- What are the characteristics of the peace Jesus leaves us/
  gives us?
- Where does the world say we will find peace? (Responses
  may include careers, bank accounts, life insurance plans,
  retirement plans, finding the perfect house, alliances with
  secular groups.)
- What does it mean that Jesus has "conquered the world"?
- How does the fact that Jesus has "conquered the world"
  encourage you and give you peace?

The following questions are of a more personal nature. Invite participants to create small groups of two to four people for this part of the
discussion. Remind the group of the covenant to keep confidentiality.
Also note that sharing is completely optional.

Distribute copies of the questions to each small group or call attention to the questions listed on a board or large sheet of paper (see "Before
the Session"). Let participants know how much time is available for this
discussion. Ask:

- In what areas of your life do you hear Jesus saying, "Don't be
  troubled or afraid?"
- What kind of peace do you long for? (in "Questions for
  Reflection" at the end of chapter 1)
- What does it mean to you to have peace in Christ?

Call the small groups back together. Read John 20:19-23. Note
that in the Gospel of John, Jesus' first and last words to the disciples are
"Peace be with you."

Read or invite a volunteer to read Ephesians 4:3-6.

Share this quotation from *Almost Christmas*:

> *Paul's words to the Ephesians address the need for unity—something we still wrestle with today. Christians in Paul's time as well as our own experience the tension between honoring our differences and looking for commonalities. It's a tension between recognizing our differences as something to celebrate rather than minimalize, and emphasizing our commonalities that draw us together. It's the need in community to find common ground without coercing people into boxes they don't belong in.*

Ask:

- Where have you experienced the tension between honoring differences and looking for commonalities among people? (You may want to apply this question to a specific context, for example our world or country, your community, or your church.)
- When have you been part of a group that celebrated diversity?

Note deVega's interpretation of Paul's teaching in Ephesians: "Even though unity is a lot easier when there is uniformity, unity from diversity is a lot closer to the heart of God." Ask:

- Why is unity from diversity closer to the heart of God?

Read or invite a volunteer to read Ephesians 4:25-32.

Call attention to deVega's observation that these instructions from Paul may be helpful to follow during holiday dinners with extended families!

Invite volunteers to read the paragraphs labeled 1–7 in the section titled "Ephesians 4: Maintaining Unity of the Spirit in the Bond of Peace." Then ask the third reflection question (which has two parts) listed at the end of chapter 1 in *Almost Christmas*.

- Which of Paul's practical instructions for peacemaking are hardest for you?
- What can you do to begin practicing them regularly?

Close this discussion by reading the last paragraph in the section titled "An Altogether Peace."

Optional Activities

An Advent Prayer Calendar

Invite participants to turn to the introduction in *Almost Christmas* and locate the list of twenty-five questions drawn from Wesley's sermon titled "The Almost Christian." Note the author's suggestion to pray through these questions, one each day, during the season of Advent "as a personal spiritual Advent calendar."

Invite participants to write the first question on a page in their notebook, journal, or electronic device. Distribute blank pieces of paper to anyone who does not have a notebook, journal, or device with them. Also, distribute pencils if needed. Offer a short time for silent prayer and journaling related to this first question. Encourage participants to continue this practice with the remaining questions during this season of Advent.

Note that there is a companion devotional titled *Almost Christmas: Devotions for the Season*, based on these twenty-five questions and select Advent hymns. Reading the devotional each day during the month of December is another way to engage with these questions prayerfully during Advent.

Silent Night

Share the stories about the hymn "Silent Night" recorded in the section of *Almost Christmas* titled "Heavenly Peace."

Play a recording of "Silent Night" or distribute hymnals so the group may sing all the verses together. After singing or listening to the hymn, ask:

- What are your favorite images or phrases in this hymn?
- Why are these meaningful for you?

Wrapping Up

Closing Activity

Read the closing paragraph of chapter 1 in the section "An Altogether Peace" in *Almost Christmas*. Ask the second reflection question listed there:

- How might you begin to seek shalom within yourself? with another person? for the world? (in "Questions for Reflection" at the end of chapter 1)

Encourage participants to continue to reflect on the question above and to read chapter 2 before the next session.

If you chose to do the Optional Activity "An Advent Prayer Calendar," remind participants to pray and journal about one of Wesley's questions each day.

Closing Prayer

Loving God of Peace, thank you for Jesus Christ who showed us how to live as peacemakers. Thank you for missionaries and teachers like the Apostle Paul and John Wesley who taught us ways to live in peace with our neighbors. Grant us wisdom, insight, and courage to follow in their footsteps and be peacemakers in our world today; in the name of your Son Jesus we pray. Amen.

SESSION 2
AN ALTOGETHER *Hope*

By INGRID MCINTYRE

Planning the Session

Session Goals

Through conversation, activities, and reflection, participants will

- identify ways we and our world need to hear a word of hope today,
- understand how John and Charles Wesley offered hope to those who felt they had no hope, and
- commit to responding to Christ's call to share hope with others.

Biblical Foundation

- 1 Peter 1:3-5

Before the Session

- Set up a table in the room with nametags, markers, Bibles, extra copies of *Almost Christmas*, and paper and pencils if any of these will be needed.
- Prepare a sign-in sheet with space for each participant's name and contact information.
- Have a markerboard or easel with paper and markers or a chalkboard and chalk available for use during the session.

- Write this question on a board or large sheet of paper for use during the "Leading into the Study" segment of the session: Who needs to hear a word of hope today?
- The Optional Activity includes instructions for your group to create a "Quilt of Hope" (a paper collage, no quilting skills required). If you would like to do this activity, write the heading "Quilt of Hope" on a board or large sheet of paper. Set up a work space with tables and chairs and the following materials:

  » pieces of paper in various colors and textures;
  » scissors, preferably at least one pair for every two or three people;
  » markers in various colors;
  » glue;
  » posterboard to be the "backing" of the quilt. If you have a large group, you may need several pieces of posterboard in order to have room for everyone's quilt pieces.

Getting Started

Greet participants as they arrive. Invite them to make a nametag and pick up either a Bible or a copy of *Almost Christmas*, or both, if they need one.

Welcome participants. If there are newcomers, allow time for introductions.

Share any items from the "Housekeeping" list in Session 1 that need repeating. Remind the group of the covenant to respect confidentiality.

Leading into the Study

Call attention to the board or large sheet of paper with this question: "Who needs to hear a word of hope today?" (see "Before the Session"). Do not offer any explanation about the question, but encourage participants to respond as they feel led. Record responses on the board or large sheet of paper. After the group has compiled the list ask:

- How many responses are for individuals?

- How many of these individuals do you know personally?
- How many groups are mentioned?
- Which individuals and groups are
  - » local?
  - » national?
  - » international?

Ask if any participants currently work with any of the groups mentioned or have worked with these groups in the past. Place an asterisk next to these groups.

Opening Prayer

Holy God of Hope, thank you for your promise of hope. Thank you for fulfilling your promise in the gift of your Son Jesus Christ. We confess that sometimes we do not see your hope. Sometimes we feel burdened by circumstances around us and we are overcome by despair and a feeling of hopelessness. Yet we know that in you there is always hope. As we journey toward Advent this year, help us move from an "Almost Hope" to an "Altogether Hope." Open our eyes to the ways you call us to bring hope to others. Grant us courage both to notice and to respond when hope is needed; in the name of your Son Jesus we pray. Amen.

Learning Together

Video Study and Discussion

Play the video for Session 2. Invite the group to consider these questions as they view the video:

- Ingrid described her ministry on the streets with people who are experiencing homelessness. How does her ministry alter her perception of hope? What do you learn from her experience?
- How are community aspects of hope different from individual, personal experiences of hope?

- April and Matt described how hope requires risk, giving us permission to envision an irrational future. What sort of irrational things do you imagine for the future? Where do you think hope is leading you to take a risk?
- Ingrid points out that Christians are not the only ones who have hope to give—we can and must receive hope from others. Where have you received hope from someone else?
- Based on the video, what would you say is the difference between an almost hope and an altogether hope?

Following the video, invite volunteers to share their responses to the questions above.

Bible Study and Discussion: 1 Peter 1:3-5

Note that dictionaries define hope as "desire accompanied by expectation of or belief in fulfillment."[1]

Highlight the fact that our hope in Christ is sure and dependable. The Apostle Paul writes, "Hope does not disappoint us, because God's love has been poured into our hearts through the Holy Spirit that has been given to us" (Romans 5:5 NRSV).

Read or invite a volunteer to read the "Biblical Foundation" text for this session, 1 Peter 1:3-5. This text as translated in the NRSV is provided at the end of chapter 2 in *Almost Christmas*.

Read the first sentence of 1 Peter 1:3 again and note that this is an acclamation of praise to God.

Then reread the second sentence in 1 Peter 1:3. As you read, give emphasis to four key concepts that give rise to the acclamation of praise, indicated here by italics:

1. By his *great mercy*
2. he has given us *a new birth*
3. into *a living hope*
4. through the *resurrection of Jesus Christ* from the dead

---

1   *Merriam-Webster*, s.v. "hope (*n.*)," accessed July 8, 2019, https://www .merriam-webster.com/dictionary/hope.

Ask:

- What does "living hope" mean to you?
- What is the "inheritance" Peter writes about in verse 4? (our salvation through Christ)

Read 1 Peter 1:4 from three different versions of the Bible as provided below. Ask participants to listen for the words that describe this "inheritance" in each version. You may want to write the descriptive words on a markerboard or large sheet of paper.

- NRSV: "an inheritance that is imperishable, undefiled, and unfading, kept in heaven for you"
- NIV: "an inheritance that can never perish, spoil or fade . . . kept in heaven for you"
- CEB: "You have a pure and enduring inheritance that cannot perish—an inheritance that is presently kept safe in heaven for you."

Ask:

- What do these descriptive words tell us about our hope and inheritance through Christ?
- What descriptive words hold the most meaning for you?
- How do we receive this inheritance? (through faith, verse 5)

Recall Paul's words in Romans 5:5 (NRSV), "hope does not disappoint us," quoted at the beginning of this "Bible Study and Discussion."

Book Study and Discussion

Invite participants to turn to the opening section of chapter 2. Ask:

- What does Ingrid McIntyre mean by an "almost hope"? (*hope for oneself*)
- Why is hope for oneself an "almost" hope rather than an "altogether" hope?

- How does McIntyre describe an "altogether hope"? (*realizing that we are "part of the whole family of Christ" and that Christ's hope is for the world*)

Call attention to the section of chapter 2 titled "Wesley: Birthing Hope" and ask:

- What was the situation in England that prompted the evangelistic work of John and Charles Wesley?
- How did John and Charles Wesley give birth to hope in places of hopelessness?

Read this sentence from John Wesley's sermon "The Marks of the New Birth." Wesley would have quoted Scripture from the KJV.

> *Thus St. Peter, speaking to all the children of God who were then scattered abroad, saith, "Blessed be the God and Father of our Lord Jesus Christ, which, according to his abundant mercy, hath begotten us again unto a lively hope."*
>
> *(1 Peter 1:3)*[2]

Note that "lively hope" is translated "living hope" in the NRSV.

Draw attention to McIntyre's point that God had been promising this "lively hope" for a long time (in the section titled "Hope and the World Upside Down"). Generations before the birth of Christ, God declared through the prophet Jeremiah: "'I know the plans I have for you,'" declares the Lord, 'plans to prosper you and not to harm you, plans to give you hope and a future'" (Jeremiah 29:11 NIV).

Invite volunteers to read these passages from the Christmas story.

Luke 1:24-25   Elizabeth

Luke 1:39-45   Mary visits Elizabeth

---

2   John Wesley, "The Sermons of John Wesley—Sermon 18: The Marks of the New Birth," Wesley Center Online, accessed July 9, 2019, http://wesley.nnu .edu/john-wesley/the-sermons-of-john-wesley-1872-edition/sermon-18-the -marks-of-the-new-birth/.

Luke 2:4-7   Mary and Joseph travel to Bethlehem, Jesus is born

Luke 2:8-12   An angel visits the shepherds

Ask:

- Why do you think God chose Elizabeth, Mary and Joseph, and the shepherds to have leading roles in the story of the birth of Jesus, the hope of the world? (Explore reasons why God's choice of these people was unexpected.)
- In what ways did Elizabeth, Mary and Joseph, and the shepherds have an "altogether hope"?
- Who are unlikely people who serve as bearers of hope to the world today?

Note McIntyre's comment: "Hope—the real thing—breaks into seemingly strange, unexpected places where people often can't afford much of anything. When we're comfortable, can we even hear the angels?"

Share this quotation from the section titled "Wesley and Altogether Hope": "Then and now, we have to be willing to show up in the strangest places, where nobody else wants to look, because that's exactly where God goes. Showing up in that way is altogether hope in action. That's exactly where Jesus is born, again and again. Those places are inside the church walls and faith traditions, *and* at homeless and refugee encampments, prisons, food pantries, protests, and political offices."

Ask the second reflection question at the end of chapter 2:

- What strange places are you willing to go for hope to be reborn? (in "Questions for Reflection")

Highlight McIntyre's observation in the section titled "Wesley: Birthing Hope" about "the difference between almost hope and altogether hope. One stands at a distance while the other relentlessly pursues; one offers platitudes while the other dives deep into the hopelessness of a situation and offers light in the darkness—light that grows and grows and grows." Ask:

31

- What experiences does McIntyre share about relentlessly pursuing hope?
- What are reasons a person would stand at a distance rather than pursue hope? (Responses may relate to fear, uncertainty, lack of understanding about God's hope, lack of awareness of ways to be bearers of hope in the world.)
- What "platitudes" have you heard, often by well-meaning people, that in reality have no power to give birth to hope?
- Where are there situations of hopelessness in your community?
- In what ways have you, your congregation, and your community responded to these situations and been agents of hope?

Ask the first reflection question at the end of chapter 2:

- Think about a situation in your life that has seemed hopeless. In what ways did you make your way through? (in "Questions for Reflection")

Call attention to McIntyre's statements in the section titled "Wesley and Altogether Hope":

- "Wesley became prophetic hope for the church."
- "Without the hope-filled prophetic voices calling us to a greater consciousness, we fail as a church."

Ask:

- What is the greater consciousness to which we are called?
- Who are prophetic voices today?

Remind participants of McIntyre's observations:

- "Despair . . . is the antithesis of hope"; and
- "Despair happens when skin doesn't show up."

Ask:

- How is hope "an antidote for despair"?

Optional Activity

Make a Quilt of Hope

Plan to do this activity during the second half of your session after the group has had the opportunity to consider some of the questions included in the "Bible Study and Discussion" and the "Book Study and Discussion."

Set up tables and place pieces of paper in various colors and textures, scissors, markers, and glue on each table. Place the posterboard on a separate table or hang on a bulletin board or wall (see "Before the Session").

Introduce this activity by sharing McIntyre's story about a quilt her mother made for her nephew, told in the section titled "Wesley and Altogether Hope":

> My mother made a quilt for my nephew, and when all of those pieces were scattered on the floor, they just looked like a jumbled mess. They were different shapes and sizes and colors. None of them looked alike. Coming together, they each carried something that made the whole quilt what it needed to be to give warmth and beauty, to tell her love story for him.
>
> I know that I am not going to end homelessness, but hope is alive in me that I can do my part and that's all God is asking. . . . Without each piece and each person, the "quilt" is not complete. As we take bold steps in hope for transformation, joining our stories with the likes of John Wesley and other faithful people, we know that one day Hope will be complete.

Prepare your group to create the quilt by inviting discussion of the following questions. Record responses on the board or large sheet of paper with the heading "Quilt of Hope" (see "Before the Session"). Ask:

- Where are situations of hopelessness in our personal lives, our church and community, our nation, and our world?
- What part can we play to bring hope to these situations?

(Responses may include prayer, specific skills, financial support, volunteer opportunities, participation in ministries such as Kairos, mission trips, and soup kitchens.)

Explain that the group will work together to create a "Quilt of Hope" that will recognize areas of hopelessness and also celebrate the ways we can be agents of hope. If you have a large group you may create several quilts.

Offer these instructions:

- Cut the pieces of paper into various shapes and sizes.
- On each piece of paper write either a situation of hopelessness or a way to offer hope. Refer to the responses to the two discussion questions above for ideas.
- Glue your quilt pieces to the posterboard in a patchwork pattern so that pieces that identify areas of hopelessness and pieces that proclaim ways we can be agents of hope are intermingled.

You may want to display your "quilt" in your church building.

Wrapping Up

Closing Activity

Ask:

- What does "an altogether hope" mean to you?
- In what ways can you embody hope for those who have been marginalized within your friends and family? within your church or social groups? within the world? (in "Questions for Reflection" at the end of chapter 2)

Encourage participants to continue to reflect on the questions above and read chapter 3 before the next session.

If you chose to do the Optional Activity in Session 1 titled "An Advent Prayer Calendar," remind participants to pray and journal about one of Wesley's questions each day.

Closing Prayer

Loving God of Hope, thank you for your Son Jesus, the fulfillment of your promise of hope for the world. Be with each of us. Open our eyes to the ways you call us to be agents of hope in places where hope seems to be lost. Let us not be overcome by despair. Fill us with courage and strength so that we may relentlessly pursue hope and be a light in the darkness; in the name of your Son Jesus we pray. Amen.

SESSION 3
AN ALTOGETHER *LOVE*

By APRIL CASPERSON

Planning the Session

Session Goals

Through conversation, activities, and reflection, participants will

- embrace God's "altogether love,"
- recognize Mary's commitment to an "altogether love," and
- understand the importance of cultivating a "private life" with God in order to grow in "altogether love."

Biblical Foundation

- Luke 1:26-45

Before the Session

- Set up a table in the room with nametags, markers, Bibles, extra copies of *Almost Christmas*, and paper and pencils if these will be needed.
- Prepare a sign-in sheet with space for each participant's name and contact information.
- Have a markerboard or easel with paper and markers or a chalkboard and chalk available for use during the session.
- Write the heading "Our Best Selves" on a board or large sheet of paper for use during "Leading into the Study."

- Have on hand four copies of the same version of the Bible to be used by the readers during the "Bible Study and Discussion." The reading will go more smoothly if the readers are following the same version.
- Draw a vertical line to create two columns on a board or large sheet of paper and write two headings, "Almost Love" and "Altogether Love." This will be used during the "Book Study and Discussion."

Getting Started

Greet participants as they arrive. Invite them to make a nametag if these are still needed and pick up either a Bible or copy of *Almost Christmas*, or both if they did not bring these.

Welcome participants. If there are newcomers, allow time for introductions.

Share any items from the "Housekeeping" list in Session 1 that need repeating. Remind the group of the covenant to respect confidentiality.

Leading into the Study

Share April Casperson's observation in the section titled "Almost Love" that "the culture in many online spaces allows and encourages us to show only our best moments publicly: the snapshot from the vacation, the staged photo of the family, a pretty picture of a sunset." Call attention to the board or large sheet of paper with the heading "Our Best Selves" and list responses to the following questions. Ask:

- What are examples of "best moments" that people are willing to share with the public, both online and in person? (Responses may relate to vacations, careers, accomplishments, awards, and relationships.)
- What are examples of personality and character traits that we are willing to reveal to others?
- Why do people want to present their best selves to the public?

Close this discussion by reading the last paragraph in the section of chapter 3 titled "Almost Love."

Opening Prayer

Holy God of Love, you love us unconditionally. You know everything about us and you still love us completely, just the way we are. Help us to trust your love for us. Open our hearts so that we may love others with an "altogether love" as you love us; in the name of your Son Jesus we pray. Amen.

Learning Together

Video Study and Discussion

Play the video for Session 3. Invite the group to consider these questions as they view the video:

- What does Mary's story teach us about what it means to love and to be loved?
- Both April and Ingrid say that altogether love is irrational. Do you agree? Why can the choice to love be irrational and scary?
- Do you agree with Magrey's idea that feeling fragmented is the opposite of love? Why or why not? What else might you describe as the opposite of love?
- What does this session say to you about the difference between an almost love and an altogether love?
- What opportunities do you see around you to experience altogether love?

Following the video, invite volunteers to share their responses to the questions above.

Bible Study and Discussion: Luke 1:26-45

Recruit four volunteers to read the "Biblical Foundation" passage for this session. Ask one volunteer to read the part of the narrator and the other volunteers to read the parts of the angel, Mary, and Elizabeth. Be sure each volunteer will be reading from the same version of the Bible as this will make it easier for them to follow their parts. Let the readers know that the passage will be read in short sections with time for discussion between the readings.

Invite the narrator, the angel, and Mary to read Luke 1:26-34. Note that Mary was "perplexed" and "pondered" (NRSV) the angel's greeting. Casperson observes that Mary stopped the angel's announcement to ask a question. Ask:

- What question did Mary ask?
- What question would you have asked?
- What does the fact that Mary "pondered" the angel's greeting tell us about her character? (Read Luke 2:19 and Luke 2:51 as part of this discussion. A key point here is that Mary observed and thought about the things that happened to her and around her. You may want to recall this aspect of Mary's personality later in the session in the discussion of the section titled "Wesley and the Private Life.")

Invite the narrator, the angel, and Mary to read Luke 1:35-38. Ask:

- What do you think gave Mary the courage to say yes to God's call for her life?
- In what ways did Mary's willingness to serve God show an "altogether love" for God?

Invite the narrator and Elizabeth to read Luke 1:39-45. Ask:

- What are reasons why Mary may have hurried to visit Elizabeth?
- What are some of the reasons Mary may have been afraid?
- How did God's "altogether love" help Mary overcome her fear and remain faithful?

Book Study and Discussion

Recruit volunteers to read the two excerpts from Wesley's sermon "The Almost Christian" provided in the section of chapter 3 titled "John Wesley and an Almost Love."

Invite participants to refer to "John Wesley and an Almost Love" during the discussion of the following questions. Ask:

- What moral, ethical, and loving acts are mentioned in these readings from Wesley's sermon?
- What might motivate a non-Christian or an "almost Christian" to practice moral, ethical, and loving acts? (*Casperson cites the examples of profit, admiration, and influence.*)
- What words and phrases does Casperson use to describe Wesley's understanding of an "almost love" as it relates to doing good things? (*"superficial," "lack of depth," and "surface level"*)

It is significant to point out here that Mary would not have been able to accept and fulfill the call to be the mother of Jesus if her love for God and humankind had been superficial and shallow.

Call attention to the board or large sheet of paper with the two headings "Almost Love" and "Altogether Love" (see "Before the Session"). Explain that participants will work together to compile a list of words and phrases that will convey the meaning of these two concepts to someone who is not familiar with the study *Almost Christmas*. Invite participants to refer to chapter 3 as a reference. Choose one of the following ways to proceed:

1. Create two groups. Ask one group to focus on "almost love" and the other group to focus on "altogether love."
2. If you have a large group, create several small groups of four to six people. Assign half of the groups "almost love" and half of the groups "altogether love."

Offer these questions to guide the discussions:

"Almost Love"
- How does a person with an "almost love" feel about himself or herself?
- How does a person with an "almost love" feel in his or her relationship with God?

- What words describe an "almost love"?

"Altogether Love"
- How does a person with an "altogether love" feel about himself or herself?
- How does a person with an "altogether love" feel in his or her relationship with God?
- What words describe an "altogether love"?

Let the groups know how much time is available for this activity. At the end of the time allotted, call the groups back together and invite each group to share. Recruit a "scribe" to record responses under the appropriate heading.

Call attention to the section of chapter 3 titled "Advent: The Now and the Not Yet" and highlight Casperson's observation that "Advent is an affirmation of the now and the not yet." Remind the group of Casperson's work at Methodist Theological School in Ohio. Ask:

- In what ways did Casperson experience "the now and not yet" as she worked with the students at this United Methodist seminary?
- Why did Casperson describe the place as "a perpetual Advent season"? (Hope lives there despite much that is unknown and uncertain.)
- What are some of the unknowns that the seminary students faced?
- What unknowns did Mary and Elizabeth face as they lived in "the now and the not yet" of God's fulfillment of God's promise of a Savior?
- In what ways are you living in "the now and the not yet"? (This question may be answered on several levels. Responses may relate to (1) hope for this Advent season; (2) hope as it pertains to aspects of daily living— for example relationships, educational and career opportunities, and healing; (3) our hope for salvation and eternal life.)

Highlight Casperson's reference to "Advent moments—moments where we saw abundant possibilities for the future without having the whole story in front of us."

Invite a volunteer to read the last paragraph of the section titled "Advent: The Now and the Not Yet." Ask:

- What words does Casperson use to describe Advent?

The following questions are more personal in nature. After you ask the questions, you may want to offer time for quiet reflection and journaling. Then invite anyone who wishes to share to do so, reminding the group of the covenant to observe confidentiality.

- How might this season of Advent be a time of regeneration and revisioning for you?
- How have you experienced the irrational nature of God's altogether love?

Draw attention to the section titled "Wesley and the Private Life." Share this quotation from this section: "For Wesley, the Christian life steeped in love had some outward signs, but the hallmark of the love of a Christian was that faithfulness was practiced in private—much like Mary's conversation with the angel and her subsequent decision to accept love and the unknown." Ask:

- In what ways do you practice faithfulness in private?
- What barriers in your faith journey have you encountered that seem to keep you at arm's length from fully embracing God's love? (in "Questions for Reflection" at the end of chapter 3)
- How do "deep, honest, private one-on-one conversations" with other people of faith help us move from an almost love to an altogether love?
- How have your times of private prayer, reflection, and devotion helped you accept God's altogether love for you?

- How have these times of private prayer, reflection, and devotion helped you move from an almost love to an altogether love for others?
- What does it mean to be fully known and loved by God?
- How does our acceptance of God's altogether love free and energize us to say yes to God's call for our lives?

Invite participants to turn to the section of chapter 3 titled "Advent and the Worship Experience." Note that Casperson contrasts the "cultural narratives" with the biblical narrative. Share this quotation: "Our call in the Advent season is to help ourselves and one another move from an almost love (a desire to control, shape, and possess a Christmas experience) into an altogether love (a reflection and experience of the mystery, danger, and abundant, unexpected life that comes to us in Christ)." Ask:

- What aspects of our culture's celebration of Christmas reveal a superficial, surface-level, almost love?
- What are you hoping for when you experience worship during this Advent season?
- In an Advent worship experience, what would help you feel fully embraced by God's altogether love? (in "Questions for Reflection" at the end of chapter 3)

Optional Activity

As a way of preparing for this Optional Activity, lead your group in compiling the lists of words and phrases that convey the meaning of "Almost Love" and "Altogether Love." Instructions for compiling these lists are included near the beginning of the "Book Study and Discussion." Then ask:

- In what ways is your church community motivated by an "almost love"?
- In what ways is your church community motivated by an "altogether love"?

- What will help your church community grow stronger in its understanding and acceptance of God's altogether love?
- How might a greater understanding and acceptance of God's altogether love influence the life of your church community?

During the discussion of these questions, encourage participants to consider outreach ministries, worship experiences, educational programs, and fellowship opportunities. Your group may want to go a step further and plan a project or program that will help their church community grow in an altogether love.

Wrapping Up

Closing Activity

Ask:

- How do you present an "almost self" to the world? What would change if you presented an "altogether self" to the world? to your church community? to God? (in "Questions for Reflection" at the end of chapter 3)

Encourage participants to continue to reflect on the questions above and read chapter 4 before the next session.

If you chose to do the Optional Activity in Session 1 titled "An Advent Prayer Calendar," remind participants to pray and journal about one of Wesley's questions each day.

Read the last paragraph in the section of chapter 3 titled "Advent, Love, and Mary's Pause."

> *Have you had experiences in your life where you stood at the beginning of a new season and said yes to love without knowing how it would all turn out? When we open ourselves to wonder and love, we are reminded that we are not the center of the universe. If our ability to be loved was rooted in our flawed selves, there is no way that we would ever be worthy of love. But God gently meets us in our imperfections, God pauses for us to ask*

45

questions, and then God welcomes us with open arms into an altogether love.

Closing Prayer

Holy and Loving God, thank you for loving us with an altogether love. Come to us in the quiet spaces of our lives so that we may grow to accept and embrace your altogether love. Let us follow the examples of Elizabeth, Mary and Joseph, and the shepherds and bear witness to your altogether love for the world; in the name of your Son Jesus we pray. Amen.

SESSION 4

AN ALTOGETHER JOY

By MATT RAWLE

Planning the Session

Session Goals

Through conversation, activities, and reflection, participants will

- discover ways the people in Luke's story of Jesus' birth experienced joy,
- consider the difference between almost joy and altogether joy, and
- recognize that God's joy is a gift.

Biblical Foundation

- Psalm 30:1-5, 11-12

Before the Session

- Set up a table in the room with nametags, markers, Bibles, and extra copies of *Almost Christmas* if these are still needed.
- Prepare a sign-in sheet with space for each participant's name and contact information.
- Have a markerboard or easel with paper and markers or a chalkboard and chalk available for use during the session.
- For the "Leading into the Study" activity:

» Draw the outline of a Christmas tree on a large piece of paper or posterboard and display it in the meeting space. A simple triangle shape will be fine, but feel free to be creative! If you have a large group, you may need more than one "tree" in order to have room for each participant to hang an "ornament" on a tree.

» Cut pieces of red and green construction paper or printer paper into circles (the circles do not need to be exact) in sizes that will resemble ornaments when taped inside the outline of the Christmas tree(s). Or provide scissors and invite early arrivers to cut out the circles. You will need enough "ornaments" for each participant to have one or two.

» Collect enough markers so each participant will have one and bring in several rolls of tape.

- Write the heading "Outline of Luke 1–2" on a board or large sheet of paper for use during the "Book Study and Discussion."

- Draw a vertical line on a board or large sheet of paper. In the first column, write the heading "Almost Joy." In the second column, write the heading "Altogether Joy." This will be used during the "Book Study and Discussion."

- If you choose to do the Optional Activity "Joy Expressed in the Psalms," you will need a list of psalms that contain the word *joy* for each small group. You may bring in several concordances to distribute among the groups or you may choose to compile a list from a concordance or online sources, or both, and make copies of the list for the groups. A few of the psalms that contain the word *joy* from an NRSV Concordance include Psalms 5, 16, 20, 21, 27, 43, 47, 51, 71, 92, 96, 98.

Getting Started

Greet participants as they arrive. Invite them to make a nametag if these are still needed, and pick up either a Bible or copy of *Almost Christmas*, or both, if they did not bring their own.

Welcome participants and if there are newcomers, allow time for introductions.

Share any items from the "Housekeeping" list in Session 1 that need repeating.

Remind the group of the covenant to respect confidentiality.

If you plan to celebrate "A Service of Covenant Renewal," remind participants of the date, time, and place. Arrange a time to meet with participants who have volunteered to assist with leadership for the service. See the instructions included with the order of service in the optional Session 5 in this Leader Guide for more information.

Leading into the Study

Call attention to the outline of the Christmas tree(s). Distribute the paper ornaments (one or two per person) and markers. Offer these instructions:

- Write one or two words on your ornament(s) that describe how you are feeling as we come to the end of this Advent season.
- Hang your ornament(s) on the tree.

After each participant has placed his or her ornament(s) on the tree, read each one without comment. Then ask:

- How many (either a number or a percentage) of these ornaments reflect joyful anticipation?
- How many ornaments reflect a sense of "I'm not ready"?
- How many ornaments reflect feelings of sadness?
- How many reflect joy?
- What other types of feelings are represented?

Opening Prayer

Holy God of Joy, we come to the end of this Advent season with a variety of feelings. We long for an altogether Christmas, complete with an altogether peace, an altogether hope, an altogether love, and an altogether joy. As we participate in the various activities that are part of our Christmas celebrations, help us remain focused on your gift of the baby Jesus, the Savior of the world; in the name of your Son Jesus we pray. Amen.

Learning Together

Video Study and Discussion

Play the video for Session 4. Invite the group to consider these questions as they view the video:

- Why is silence sometimes required for us to experience an altogether joy?
- What does an altogether joy look like for someone who is not experiencing happiness or is going through a hard time during the Advent and Christmas season?
- Based on the conversation in the video, what would you say is the difference between joy and happiness? How does an altogether joy go beyond happiness?
- Do you agree that the opposite of joy is a feeling of being stuck? Why or why not?
- Matt describes joy as the steadfast assurance that God is with us. Where do you feel that kind of assurance? How does it bring you joy?

Following the video, invite volunteers to share their responses to the questions above.

Bible Study and Discussion: Psalm 30:1-5, 11-12

Invite participants to read Psalm 30:1-5 (NRSV) together, as provided in *Almost Christmas*. Then read Psalm 30:11-12 (NRSV):

> You have turned my mourning into dancing;
>> you have taken off my sackcloth
>> and clothed me with joy,
> so that my soul may praise you and not be silent.
>> O LORD my God, I will give thanks to you forever.

Say:

- In verse 2 the psalmist praises God for healing, but the specific type of healing is not stated.
- Matt Rawle points out that the cause of the psalmist's suffering is not as important as the fact that the psalmist recognizes that God is the one who draws him up.
- In verse 3 "Sheol" and "the Pit" refer to the place of the dead.

Read the first part of verse 1 from three different versions of the Bible as provided below and invite participants to listen for variations in wording:

- NRSV: "I will extol you, O LORD, for you have drawn me up."
- CEB: "I exalt you, LORD, because you pulled me up."
- NIV: "I will exalt you, LORD, for you lifted me out of the depths."

Ask:

- In verse 4 how does the psalmist respond to God's healing? (He sings praises, gives thanks, and calls God's "faithful ones" [NRSV] to join him.)
- In verses 5 and 11, what does the psalmist tell us about God?

Note that in verse 12 the psalmist again offers praise and thanksgiving to God.

Invite participants to reflect silently for a minute about a time they called upon God for help and God drew them up or lifted them out of the depths. Ask:

- How do you offer praise and thanksgiving to God when God has answered your prayers for help? (It is not necessary for participants to share information about the circumstances they have in mind. These may be very personal. Focus the conversation on the ways we respond to God's help and healing.)

Share Rawle's comment, "What I love about this psalm is the honesty that joy is a gift, and this gift is often in the context of great despair and sadness."

Reread these phrases from Psalm 30 (NRSV):

- "Weeping may linger for the night, but joy comes with the morning" (verse 5).
- "You have turned my mourning into dancing; you have taken off my sackcloth and clothed me with joy" (verse 11).

Ask:

- What do these phrases tell us about joy?
- When have you experienced joy as the psalmist did?

Book Study and Discussion

Invite participants to turn to the first chapter of the Gospel of Mark. Ask:

- What is the first event Mark records in the life of John the Baptist? (*his preaching and baptizing in the wilderness*)
- What is the first event Mark records in the life of Jesus? (*his baptism by John*)

Read the first paragraph under the section titled "A Fleeting, Almost Joy" in chapter 4 about the Gospel of Mark or summarize Rawle's comments about this Gospel, noting his statement that Mark is "fast-paced and action-packed." Ask:

- In what ways has your celebration of this Advent season been "fast paced and action packed"?

Invite participants to skim the first two chapters of the Gospel of Luke and identify the events Luke records surrounding the birth of Jesus. As the group identifies the various parts of the story, write them in outline form on a board or large sheet of paper including chapter and verse.

If you have a large group, create small groups of four to six people for this activity. Let the groups know how much time is available for making the outlines. Call the groups back together and compare findings. The completed outline will look something like this:

- The angel visits Zechariah in the temple   Luke 1:5-23
- Elizabeth   Luke 1:24-25
- The angel appears to Mary   Luke 1:26-38
- Mary visits Elizabeth   Luke 1:39-45
- Mary's "Magnificat"   Luke 1:46-56
- Elizabeth gives birth to John   Luke 1:57-66
- Zechariah's prophecy   Luke 1:67-80
- Journey to Bethlehem and Jesus' birth   Luke 2:1-7
- The angel appears to the shepherds   Luke 2:8-14
- The shepherds visit the baby Jesus   Luke 2:15-20
- Jesus' parents fulfill the Law   Luke 2:21-24
- Simeon in the temple   Luke 2:25-35
- Anna in the temple   Luke 2:36-40

Consider the people in Luke's story of Jesus' birth in turn—Zechariah, Elizabeth, Mary, Joseph, the shepherds, Simeon, and Anna—and for each one ask:

- Where did Luke indicate pauses and space in which this person/group experienced the joy of the birth of Jesus?
- How did this person/group respond to or express joy over the birth of Jesus?

Summarize Rawle's story about a "Longest Night" service and read his concluding sentence about this experience: "Although I can't conceive how you might place this under a tree, silence is sometimes the very gift we need for joy to be experienced."

Also share his observation about joy in Luke's Gospel: "In Luke's Gospel, joy comes after silence, and it is experienced in the midst of persecution. This is a far cry from what we typically recognize as joy during the Advent and Christmas season. Joy certainly can be happy and cheerful, but this 'almost joy' misses the fullness of what Scripture seems to say about the joy we feel as followers of Christ." Ask:

- When have you experienced joy within the silence?
- When have you experienced joy during or after times of trial, suffering, and hardship?

The two questions above are of a personal nature. You may want to remind the group of the covenant to observe confidentiality before the discussion. If you have a large group, invite participants to share in pairs or groups of three or four people so everyone who wants to share will have the opportunity.

Invite participants to sing the hymn "Hark! the Herald Angels Sing" written by Charles Wesley. The words to the first verse are provided in chapter 4. You may want to bring in hymnals and sing all the verses (*The United Methodist Hymnal*, 240).

Suggest that participants refer to Rawle's comments about this hymn as they respond to the following questions. Ask:

- What did John and Charles Wesley understand to be the source of our joy? ("*God and sinners reconciled!*")
- Why is there no joy for those who do not feel forgiveness or assurance of salvation?
- Why does Rawle say, "Without joy there is little for which to give thanks"?
- In what ways are mercy and grace related to joy?

Remind the group that the four candles on the Advent wreath represent Peace, Hope, Love, and Joy. Share Rawle's observations about these candles:

- "Joy is the culmination of our Advent celebration because joy is a gift.
- Hope is a future destination for which we dream and work.
- Peace is a daily discipline to put down the sword in whatever form it is known.
- Love requires a selflessness in order to be shared.

- Joy is different from the other candles we light during the season because joy cannot be achieved. Joy simply is a gift."

Draw attention to the board or large sheet of paper with the headings "Almost Joy" and "Altogether Joy" (see "Before the Session"). Invite participants to refer to chapter 4 and also personal experience as they respond to these questions. Record responses in the appropriate column. Ask:

- What words describe "Almost Joy"? Or, what is "Almost Joy"?
- What words describe "Altogether Joy"? Or, what is "Altogether Joy"? (Remind the group of Rawle's observation that "sometimes joy is indescribable.")

Share these quotations from the last two paragraphs in the section titled "Indescribable Joy."

- "Experiencing joy and experiencing God are one and the same."
- "Joy is the steadfast assurance that God is with us.... There's nothing else we need to know."

Ask:

- How do these two statements ring true for your experience of joy?

Optional Activities

An Advent Prayer Calendar

If you chose to do the Optional Activity in Session 1 titled "An Advent Prayer Calendar," offer time for participants to share their experiences of praying through John Wesley's twenty-five questions.

Joy Expressed in the Psalms

Invite participants to create small groups of four to eight people. Provide each group with a concordance or list of psalms that contain the word *joy* (see "Before the Session"). Instruct the groups to select and read several psalms about joy and respond to these questions:

- What does this psalm tell us about joy?
- What was the psalmist's experience of joy?
- How is the psalmist's experience similar to or different from my experience of joy?

Call the groups back together and offer time for each group to share their findings.

Wrapping Up

Closing Activity

Invite participants to reflect for a moment about the four sessions you have shared together. Then ask:

- In what ways has this study helped you move from celebrating an Almost Christmas to celebrating an Altogether Christmas?

If you plan to celebrate "A Service of Covenant Renewal," remind the group of the necessary information about the service.

Closing Prayer

Holy God, we thank you for the gift of the Christ Child at Christmas, the Prince of Peace, the hope of the world, your gift of love, and the source of our joy. As we journey from this season of Advent to the celebration of Christmas, we pray for your constant presence. Open our hearts to receive your abundant gifts. Open our hearts to share your abundant gifts, that we may be peacemakers and bearers of hope in the world, that we may love you and others with an altogether love, and that we may truly experience your gift of joy; in the name of your Son Jesus we pray. Amen.

SESSION 5 (OPTIONAL)

A SERVICE OF
*C*OVENANT RENEWAL

You may decide to close your study of *Almost Christmas* with "A Service of Covenant Renewal" as described in the closing section of the epilogue of *Almost Christmas*: "An Altogether Commitment: Wesleyan Covenant Renewal." Guidelines and suggestions for such a service are outlined below. This service is based on a covenant renewal service written by John Wesley.

Decide when you would like to have the service. It is appropriate to celebrate this service around the start of a new year. One option is to schedule the service on your regular meeting day and time soon after the New Year holiday. You may also choose a different day, such as New Year's Eve or New Year's Day or the first Sunday in January.

The service includes the Sacrament of Holy Communion. If you are not an ordained elder, invite an ordained elder to come and lead this part of the service. You may want to ask a member of the church worship team to help you make arrangements for securing and serving the Communion elements of bread and grape juice.

The three hymns included in the order of service are by Charles Wesley. Recruit a pianist or organist and have hymnals on hand. Make a note of the hymn numbers before the service.

As facilitator for the class, you may want to read the parts designated "Leader" yourself. You may invite participants in your group to read Scripture, lead the hymns, and assist with serving Holy Communion.

In part 3 you will see "Sermon or other word of witness." The sermon may be based on the Scripture passages that are read or topics included in the book *Almost Christmas*. You may choose to

- deliver the sermon yourself;
- invite someone else to deliver the sermon;
- invite one or more participants in your group to share words of witness, based either on their experience of the study *Almost Christmas* or on some other circumstances as appropriate.

Reserve the space where you would like to hold the service. You may want to hold the service in your church sanctuary or chapel. Another option is to hold the service in your meeting space. If you do this, set up a table to serve as the altar with a cloth, cross, candles, a Bible, and the elements for Holy Communion. You will also need a piano and hymnbooks.

Each participant will need a copy of the order of worship provided below that includes the prayers and responses of the people. The order of worship is included as an appendix in *Almost Christmas*, so participants may use their copy of the book for this purpose. Be sure to remind everyone to bring their books with them to the service. Alternatively, you may type and print these as bulletins to hand out to people as they arrive for the service. If you need help from church staff in typing and printing these bulletins, make arrangements for this in advance.

A SERVICE OF COVENANT RENEWAL

From *One Faithful Promise*
by Magrey R. deVega
Based on "Directions for Renewing Our Covenant with God"
by John Wesley (1780)

Gathering

Call to Worship

LEADER: This covenant I advise you to make, not only in heart, but in word; not only in word, but in writing; and that you would with all possible reverence spread the writing before the Lord, as if you would present it to him as your act and deed: and when you have done this, set your hand to it: keep it as a memorial of the solemn transactions that have passed between God and you, that you may have recourse to it in doubts and temptations.

Opening Prayer

PEOPLE: O Most Holy God, for the sake of your Son, Jesus Christ, we offer ourselves to you as prodigals at your doorstep. We have fallen short because of our sins, and are prone to the wickedness and evil in the world. But you have promised mercy to us in Christ, and you call us to turn to you with all of our hearts. Therefore, by the call of your gospel, we come now, without reluctance, to submit ourselves to your mercy.

Opening Hymn
"A Charge to Keep I Have"

1. We Confide in God

LEADER: Having a full, life-giving relationship with God means putting away our idols, and being against that which God is against. Therefore, renounce those things from the bottom of your hearts, and in full covenant, use all the means that you know to refuse sin and corruption in your lives.

PEOPLE: O God, though we once were of the world, we now resign our hearts to you, humbly bowing before your majesty, with firm resolution in our hearts.

Scripture Reading

One or more of the following passages of Scripture are read: Jeremiah 31:31-34; Luke 9:18-27; 1 Peter 1:13-25; Colossians 3:1-14.

2. We Compose Our Spirits

Prayer of Confession and Assurance of Pardon

LEADER: Let us pray.

PEOPLE: O God, we wholeheartedly desire your grace, so that we might follow your call with resolve, forsake the world, turn away from sin, and turn to you. We will guard against all

temptations, in good times and bad, lest they draw us away from you. We acknowledge our own powerlessness against such forces, and rely on your righteousness and strength.

(Silent prayer of confession)

LEADER: God is boundless in mercy and great grace, and offers us again to be our God through Christ. Therefore we solemnly pledge ourselves to God, bowing before God's majesty.

PEOPLE: We take you as our Lord Jehovah, Father, Son, and Holy Spirit. We yield our whole selves, body and soul, for your service, promising and vowing to serve you in holiness and righteousness every day of our lives.

Passing of the Peace

(Signs of peace and reconciliation are exchanged.)

Hymn of Preparation
"Come Let Us Use the Grace Divine"

3. We Claim the Covenant

Sermon or Other Word of Witness

Prayer of Commitment

LEADER: Since God has given Jesus as the only way to God, solemnly accept Jesus as the only new and living way, by which sinners may come to God. I call you to join in covenant with God.

PEOPLE: (The following is prayed in silence.) O blessed Jesus, I come to you hungry, wretched, miserable, blind, and naked. I am tarnished by sin, and my uncleanliness makes me unable to be in a relationship with you. But your love for me is unparalleled, so with all my heart I accept you, and take you to be my Lord, for richer and for poorer, for all times and conditions, to love, honor, and obey before all others, until my death. I embrace you in every way, renouncing my sinfulness, my wisdom, and my will, offering myself fully to you and taking your will to govern my life. And since you told me that I will suffer if I try to do this alone, I enter into a covenant with you, come what may. Your grace will assist me when I run into trouble, and I know that nothing in life or death will separate me from you.

The Wesley Covenant Prayer

LEADER: Let us pray this covenant prayer in the Wesleyan tradition.

PEOPLE: I am no longer my own, but thine.
Put me to what thou wilt, rank me with whom thou wilt.
Put me to doing, put me to suffering.
Let me be employed for thee or laid aside for thee,
exalted for thee or brought low for thee.
Let me be full, let me be empty.
Let me have all things, let me have nothing.
I freely and heartily yield all things to thy pleasure and disposal.

And now, O glorious and blessed God, Father, Son, and Holy Spirit,
thou art mine, and I am thine. So be it.
And the covenant which I have made on earth,
let it be ratified in heaven. Amen.

Sacrament of Holy Communion

4. We Choose Faithfulness

Prayer of Commitment

O God, Because you have been pleased to give your holy law as the rule of my life and the way I should walk in your kingdom, I willingly submit myself to you, set my shoulder to your burden, and subscribe in all your laws as holy, just, and good. I solemnly take them, as the rule of my words, thoughts, and actions, promising that though my flesh might contradict and rebel, I will try to order and govern my whole life according to your direction, and will not allow myself to neglect any of my duties to you. Now, Almighty God, searcher of hearts, you know that I make this covenant with you today without deceit or reservation, asking you, that if you see any flaw or falsehood in me, that you would reveal it to me and help me to get right with you.

Closing Hymn
"Jesus, United by Thy Grace"

5. We Connect to God in Prayer

LEADER: And now, glory be to you, O God the Father.

PEOPLE: From this day forward I look upon you as my God and Father, knowing that you are always looking for ways to recover sinners like me.

LEADER: Glory be to you, O God the Son.

PEOPLE: You have loved me and washed me from my sins in your own blood, and you are my Savior and Redeemer.

LEADER: Glory be to you, O God the Holy Spirit. By the power of your hand, you have turned my heart away from sin and back to you.

ALL: O holy and powerful God, Father, Son, and Holy Spirit, you are now my Covenant-Friend, and through your infinite grace, I am your Covenant-Servant. Amen. So be it. And the covenant which I have made on earth, let it be ratified in heaven.

Benediction

Depart in Peace